The Life of
W. K. Kellogg

Tiffany Peterson

www.heinemann.co.uk/library

To order:
☎ Phone 44 (0) 1865 888066
▤ Send a fax to 44 (0) 1865 314091
▭ Visit the Heinemann Bookshop at www.heinemann.co.uk/library to browse our catalogue and order online.

First published in Great Britain by Heinemann Library, Halley Court, Jordan Hill, Oxford OX2 8EJ, part of Harcourt Education.
Heinemann is a registered trademark of Harcourt Education Ltd.

© Harcourt Education Ltd 2003
First published in paperback in 2004.
The moral right of the proprietor has been asserted.

Editorial: Angela McHaney Brown, Kathy Peltan
Design: Herman Adler Design
Map Illustrations: Mapping Specialists
Picture Research: Carol Parden
Production: Edward Moore

Originated by QueNet™
Printed and bound in China by South China Printing Company

ISBN 0 431 18072 5 (hardback)
07 06 05 04 03
10 9 8 7 6 5 4 3 2 1

ISBN 0 431 18077 6 (paperback)
07 06 05 04
10 9 8 7 6 5 4 3 2 1

British Library Cataloguing in Publication Data
Peterson, Tiffany
    The Life of W. K. Kellogg
    338.7'664756'092
A full catalogue record for this book is available from the British Library.

Acknowledgements
The Publishers would like to thank the following for permission to reproduce photographs: Unless otherwise noted images provided by Kellogg Company, Kellogg's Cereal City, USA, and W. K. Kellogg Foundation. Used with permission.

Cover, pp. 1, 4 Brian Warling/Heinemann Library.

Special thanks to Michelle Rimsa for her comments in the preparation of this book.

Disclaimer
All the Internet addresses (URLs) given in this book were valid at the time of going to press. However, due to the dynamic nature of the Internet, some addresses may have changed, or sites may have changed or ceased to exist since publication. While the author and the Publishers regret any inconvenience this may cause readers, no responsibility for any such changes can be accepted by either the author or the Publishers.

Contents

Any words in bold, **like this**, are explained in the Glossary

Cereal for breakfast

Cold cereal is a popular breakfast food. You may have had it for breakfast this morning. Kellogg's cereals are made and eaten all over the world.

Kellogg's brand cereals come in a wide variety of flavours.

Cereal flakes were **invented** by accident in the USA in the late 1800s by two brothers, Will Keith (W. K.) and John Harvey Kellogg.

W. K. was working for his brother when they made the first wheat-flake cereal.

The early years

W. K. helped on his father's farm every day after school. In this family photo, W. K. is the child in the centre.

W. K. Kellogg was born on 7 April 1860, in Battle Creek, Michigan. He did not do very well at school. He could not see the **blackboard** because he needed glasses.

When he was fourteen, W. K. left school. He worked as a salesperson in his father's broom company. He became good at business.

When he was nineteen, W. K. went to Texas to help run a broom **factory**.

Back to Michigan

W. K. worked in the state of Texas for one year. In 1879, he returned to Michigan and married Ella Osborn Davis. She had also grown up in Battle Creek.

W. K. had known Ella for many years before they got married.

W. K. was often home only when his children were asleep. Elizabeth, John and Karl are shown here.

W. K. and Ella had four sons and a daughter. W. K. always worked long hours, so he did not have much time to spend with his wife and children.

A new job

W. K. went to work for his brother, John Harvey, from 1880. John Harvey was a doctor and ran the Battle Creek Sanitorium (the San). This was like a hospital and a holiday place.

The nickname for John Harvey's sanitorium was 'the San'.

W. K. handled the money for the San. He also did small jobs, such as shining John Harvey's shoes. W. K. worked hard, but he was unhappy with his job.

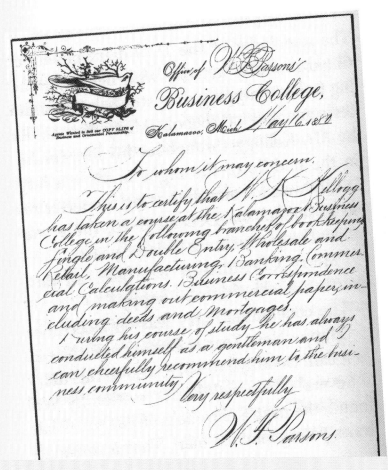

W. K. wanted to be successful, so he went to college to study business. This is his **certificate**.

Breakfast foods

The San did not serve tea, coffee or **spicy** food.

John Harvey served simple foods at the San. Patients did not think it had much taste. So John Harvey asked W. K. to help him find a tasty, healthy breakfast food.

By chance, W. K. left a pot of boiled wheat sitting for two days. When the brothers rolled the mushy wheat flat, it came out in flakes. When toasted then cooled, the flakes tasted quite good.

This museum display shows W. K. and John Harvey on the day they first made wheat flakes.

A new business

John Harvey served the toasted wheat flakes for breakfast at the San. People liked this new food. People even wanted to eat the cereal back at home.

The Kellogg brothers sold their cereal through the San's food company.

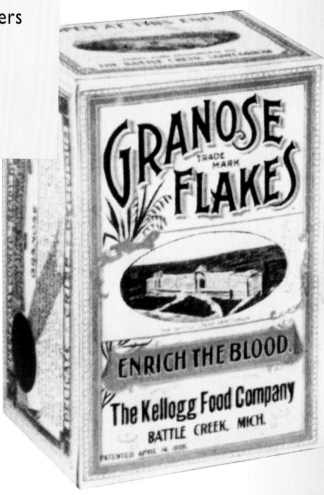

People who had never been to the San began ordering the cereal.

W. K. was put in charge of his brother's new food business. He worked hard to make the business grow. He **advertised** in newspapers and magazines.

On his own

W. K. **experimented** to make the cereal better. He tried using corn instead of wheat. Then he added a little sugar.

W. K. found that sugar made both corn and wheat flakes taste better.

John Harvey did not want to add sugar to food. So W. K. started his own company. It was called the Battle Creek Toasted Corn Flake Company.

W. K. opened his first **factory** in 1906 in Battle Creek, behind the San.

Other cereals

The Kelloggs made people interested in cereal. During the early 1900s, more than 40 companies in Battle Creek were selling wheat-flake cereal.

Battle Creek in Michigan became known as the cereal capital of the world.

One of these other companies was also successful. C. W. Post had stayed at the San. He started the Post Cereal Company, and it is still successful today.

This picture shows the first Post Cereal office headquarters.

Success!

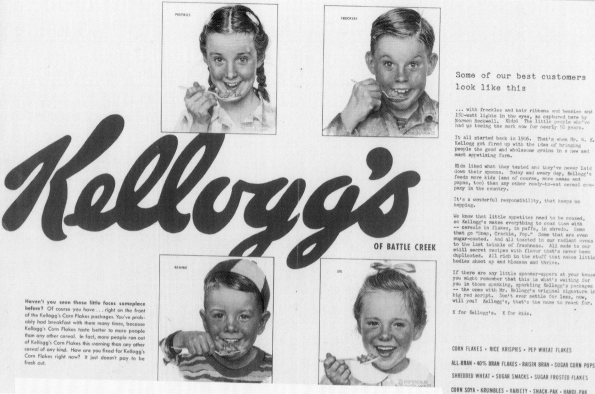

Some ads offered free cereal to anyone who asked for Kellogg's cereal in a shop.

W. K. had to get people to buy his cereal instead of the **imitations**. He knew the key was getting shops to sell it. He turned again to **advertising**.

W. K.'s advertisements were a success. Toasted **Corn Flakes** were soon being sold all around the country.

The name of W.K.'s company was changed to Kellogg's in 1907.

The Largest Electric Sign Ever Built

THE above photograph shows the monster Kellogg Toasted Corn Flake electric sign on the top of the Mecca Building, at 48th and Broadway, New York.

This sign is 106 feet wide and 80 feet high—the letter "K" in Kellogg's is 66 feet high—the boy's head and the package are 40 feet high.

Eighty tons of structural iron were required for the frame work, making necessary six mammoth trusses to distribute the weight and wind stress over the building.

A mechanical device changes the boy's face and the heading. When he cries the heading reads "I want Kellogg's." He then smiles and the heading reads "I got Kellogg's." The sign portrays a true story told in millions of homes daily.

W. K. Kellogg

THE ORIGINAL HAS THIS SIGNATURE

A friendly boss

W. K. was a good boss. He wanted people to work hard, but he treated them well. When his **factory** burned down in 1907, W. K. kept paying his workers.

W. K. paid his workers to help rebuild the burnt factory.

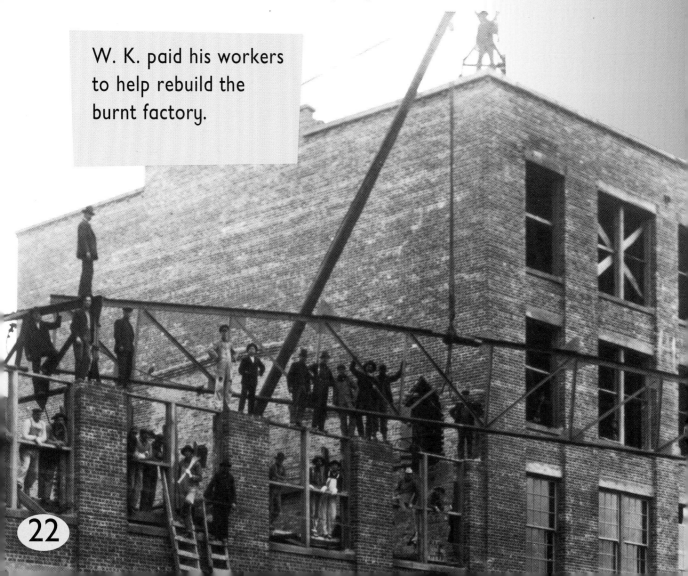

W. K. often visited the workers in his cereal factory. He also tested new equipment.

If W. K. heard that one of his workers could not pay for a doctor, he would secretly pay the bill himself.

Caring for others

W. K.'s wife, Ella, died in 1912. He kept busy working on making better cereal. Six years later, he married his second wife, Carrie.

Dr Carrie Staines worked at the San. That is where she and W. K. met.

W. K.'s company made him rich. He used his money to help people. He gave money so poor children could go to the doctor. He also built schools and summer camps.

Summer camps, such as this one, gave healthy holidays to poor children.

A school for all

This school was the first to teach together children who did and did not have special needs.

W. K. started the Ann J. Kellogg School, named after his mother. Any child could go to the school. Some children at the school had trouble seeing, hearing or walking.

In his mid-60s, W. K. learned he had an eye problem called **glaucoma**. By 1942, he was blind. W. K. died on 6 October, 1951. He was 91 years old.

W. K.'s guide dog helped him move around as his sight failed.

Learning more about W. K. Kellogg

W. K. Kellogg is remembered not only as the **inventor** of cold cereals. He is also remembered as a kind and helpful man.

At the Cereal City USA museum in Battle Creek, visitors can learn more about W. K. Kellogg's life.

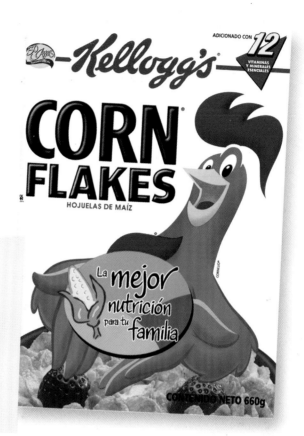

Kellogg's products are sold in 160 countries. The labelling on this box is in Spanish.

Today, Kellogg's is the world's top cereal maker. The company has **factories** in nineteen countries. The W. K. Kellogg **Foundation** continues W. K.'s work in helping people.

Fact file

- W. K. took steps to help protect wildlife and the environment, as well as working with people.
- The main office of the Kellogg's Company is still in Battle Creek, Michigan, USA.
- At the Michigan Historical Museum in Lansing, Michigan, visitors can learn more about the cereal boom in Battle Creek.
- All his life, W. K. liked horses. He built a home in California where he kept 30 horses.
- In 1994 a college for adult learners at Oxford University, founded by the Kellogg Foundation, was named Kellogg College.

Timeline

7 April 1860	W. K. Kellogg is born in Battle Creek, Michigan, USA
1880	W. K. marries Ella Osborn Davis and goes to work for his brother at the Battle Creek Sanitorium (the San)
1894	W. K. and his brother discover how to make wheat flakes
1906	W. K. starts his own cereal business – the Battle Creek Toasted Corn Flake Company
1907	W. K. changes the name of the company to Kellogg's
1912	Ella Osborn Kellogg dies
1918	W. K. marries Dr Carrie Staines
6 October 1951	W. K. Kellogg dies

Glossary

advertise to tell people about something so they will buy it

blackboard board at the front of a classroom, on which a teacher writes with chalk

certificate official letter that says someone has completed school

corn flakes cold cereal made from corn that has been cooked and rolled into flakes

experiment to test in order to discover or prove something

factory place where a large amount of something is made

foundation organization set up to help fund good causes, like education and children's charities

glaucoma eye problem that can cause blindness

imitation something that copies something else

invent make something that has never been made before

spicy having a strong flavour

More books to read

Look After Yourself: Healthy Food, Angela Royston, (Heinemann Library, 2003)

Safe and Sound: Eat Well, Angela Royston, (Heinemann Library, 2000)

Index